TIME TO CHANGE THE 1981 EDUCATION ACT

THE LONDON FILE - PAPERS FROM THE
INSTITUTE OF EDUCATION
Titles in the series include:

WHAT WE KNOW ABOUT EFFECTIVE PRIMARY TEACHING   Caroline Gipps

MORE HAS MEANT WOMEN: The feminisation of schooling   Jane Miller

THE ARTS 5-16: Changing the agenda   John White

MUSIC EDUCATION AND THE NATIONAL CURRICULUM   Keith Swanwick

NATIONAL CURRICULUM SCIENCE: So near and yet so far   Arthur Jennings

THE AIMS OF SCHOOL HISTORY: The National Curriculum and beyond

Peter Lee, Denis Shemilt, John Slater, Paddy Walsh and John White

THE PROMISE AND PERILS OF EDUCATIONAL COMPARISON   Martin McLean

For a complete list of the London File Papers please write to
The Tufnell Press,
47 Dalmeny Road,
London,
N7 0DY

THE LONDON FILE
PAPERS FROM THE INSTITUTE OF EDUCATION

TIME TO CHANGE
THE 1981
EDUCATION ACT

BRAHM NORWICH

INSTITUTE OF
EDUCATION
UNIVERSITY OF LONDON

Published by

the Tufnell Press

THE LONDON FILE - PAPERS FROM THE INSTITUTE OF EDUCATION

PUBLISHED
by
the Tufnell Press
47, Dalmeny Road, London, N7 0DY

© 1992, Brahm Norwich

First published 1992

BRITISH LIBRARY CATALOGUING-IN-PUBLICATION DATA
A catalogue record for this book is available from the British Library

ISBN 1 872767 36 2

Book design by Fiona Barlow, Carter Wong, London
Printed in Great Britain by Da Costa Print, London

CONTENTS

INTRODUCTION

This pamphlet is about the need for changes to the current legislation dealing with special educational needs in England and Wales—the Education Act, 1981. It is nine years since the Act was implemented and since then there have been some basic changes in the national education system, in particular the Education Reform Act, 1988. Few people would have anticipated in the late 1970s and early 1980s, when the 1981 Act was drafted and legislated, the breadth and depth of changes which the education system is currently undergoing. It is now time to reconsider the 1981 Act in the light of its operation in these circumstances and in the context of the far reaching proposals contained in the recent *Choice and Diversity* White paper (DFE, 1992b).

In the wake of the recent Audit Commission/HMI report on special education provision (Audit Commission/HMI, 1992) and with its recent proposals for amendments to the procedures associated with statutory assessment and Statementing (DFE, 1992a), the Government plans to amend the 1981 Act in the near future. This pamphlet will discuss some aspects of the 1981 Act from a number of perspectives which focus on the basic principles and framework of policy and practice in this field. It was not written originally as a response to these proposals, though much of the content is relevant to them. It was planned about a year ago before the recent Government proposals were even envisaged. It is hoped that some of the suggestions will be relevant to understanding some possible future difficulties associated with the White Paper and 1981 Act amendment proposals.

BACKGROUND

Compatibility of the 1981 and 1988 Acts

Much has been said about the incompatibility of the 1981 and the 1988 Acts. Some of the initial apprehensions about the Education Reform Act were that it took little account of pupils with special educational needs and that its effects would be to undo some of the positive developments which had been reinforced by and initiated following the 1981 Act. Further consideration has led to the view that there was a compatibility problem in the underlying principles of the two pieces of legislation. This view (Wedell, 1990) has questioned whether the 1988 Act has or will promote the development of good practice in terms of several key principles said to be associated with the 1981 Act:

* Special educational needs are no longer seen as caused solely by factors *within* the child. They are recognised as the outcome of the interaction between the strengths and weaknesses of the child and the resources and deficiencies of the child's environment.
* It is therefore not meaningful or even possible to draw a clear dividing line which separates the 'handicapped' from the 'non-handicapped'. Special educational needs occur across a continuum of degree.
* All children are entitled to education. The aims of education are the same for all children, but the means by which the aims can be attained differ, as does the extent to which they may be achieved.
* All schools have a responsibility to identify and meet children's special educational needs, and all children should be educated with their peers as long as their needs can be met, and it is practicable to do so. (Wedell, 1990, p.2)

It is not easy to identify summary parallel principles associated with the Education Reform Act as there are several different aspects to this substantial piece of legislation. However, as regards the National Curriculum it is possible to identify a principle from *From Policy to Practice* (DES, 1989b):

The principle that each pupil should have a broad and balanced curriculum which is also relevant to his or her particular needs is now established in law.

The National Curriculum Council (NCC) has also affirmed:

> full support for the principle of maximum participation in the National
> Curriculum by all pupils with special educational needs and for the minimal
> use of exceptional arrangements which are available through section 17-19
> of the Education Reform Act, 1988. (National Curriculum Council, 1989)

From the point of view of schooling, the 1988 Act can be seen as embodying
two main principles. One is concerned with a national common framework with
a set of arrangements for what is taught and how attainment is assessed; a
centralising principle. The other principle was concerned with a 'market' choice
principle. This involves giving the users of the school service more choice in the
selection of schools, by more open enrolment of school, a wider variety of schools
and by the introduction of grant maintained schools (GMS), 'opting out' of LEAs.
This is put forward in the Parent's Charter on education (DES, 1991a) as a 'right
to choose'. Connected to this is a 'right to know', which includes amongst other
things, information for parents about their child's progress and comparable
performance tables of local schools in terms of the National Curriculum assessments.
The second strand to the 'market' choice principle involved the introduction of
local management of schools (LMS); a system of delegating financial and managerial
responsibilities to school governing bodies. LMS was designed to increase the
accountability and responsiveness of schools to their users, as stated in Circular 7/
91 on LMS, the aim was to give:

> ...schools more autonomy in the management of resources and making
> headteachers and governors more accountable to parents, pupils and local
> communities. (DES 1991b, para.2)

These principles have been reinforced by the recent White Paper (DFE, 1992b).

Although much has been said about irreconcilable differences in the principles
associated with the 1988 and 1981 Acts, the differences between the two Act are
not exactly clear. Both Acts can be seen as consistent with the principle of a
common curriculum framework and entitlement for all children. Similarly, the
principle that schools have more financial and management responsibility is
compatible with their taking responsibility for including more children with
special educational needs; it is even a necessary condition. This suggests that it is
not a difference in these principles, but rather the ways in which the National

Curriculum and LMS principles have been formulated and put into operation which sets up a tension between the two Acts.

The 1988 Act version of a national curriculum was designed mainly for national assessment and reporting purposes; accountability purposes. This has required the construction of a national system of assessment, enabling comparisons of attainment between pupils and between schools. This has meant that little effort went into developing more general learning intentions for children from an explicit conception of what was worth learning (O'Hear and White, 1990). By building the design around ten subjects, divided into many attainment targets each with ten levels of attainment, the Act is strongly prescriptive and makes considerable demands on schools and teachers in relation to content, assessment and the reporting of attainment. This has taken no account of the need for flexibility and choice in the specific form of the National Curriculum and its implementation; something with special relevance to the inclusion of all children, particularly those with special educational needs, within a common curriculum framework. This prescriptive approach was required by the Government's plan to produce consumer information about educational standards, reflecting its commitment to the principle of individual consumer 'market' choice. Underlying this commitment is the key assumption that introducing such choice will improve the education service in this country. It is this uncritical acceptance of an individual 'market' version of a choice principle which is the major flaw in the Government's position. This version of the individual choice principle reduces the degree of autonomy and influence of teachers and schools to affect the actual form and content of the school curriculum.

Similarly, the specific version of LMS adopted by the Government has been based on maximising the amount of finance delegated to individual schools, based on the number of children at the school. This sets up a quasi-market system whereby individual parental choice of the school affects the school's grant. The effect of this, with the powers of schools to become grant maintained now reinforced by the White Paper proposals, reduces the capability of any agency, whether LEA or the proposed Funding Agency for Schools (FAS) to plan and coordinate an education service from the wider perspective and interests of the local citizens. This reduced local capability has considerable significance for the operation of the 1981 Act, as this Act depends on the role of such an agency in relation to ordinary and special schools.

4

Local agency role

The fundamental role of the LEA is to identify pupils whose needs cannot be met through generally available provision in ordinary schools and to ensure that additional or different provision is made available. However, with a combination of schools having to report their attainment levels publicly, with funding affected by individual parental choice and with finances being tight, schools will find it harder to take responsibility for pupils with special educational needs. In 1988 this was expected to lead, and as recent reports show it is leading, to more school pressures on LEAs to take responsibility for making additional or different provision (Audit Commission/HMI 1992). Yet, LEAs, with increasing delegation of funds to schools and their own declining role, have less means to enable schools to take more responsibility for pupils with special educational needs.

So, it can be seen how the current version of LMS reflects the Government's commitment to individual consumer 'market' choice without balancing this with an enabling and regulating role for organisations like LEAs or the proposed Funding Agency for Schools. From the special educational needs perspective, this weakens the LEAs' capability to influence the special educational needs policy and practice of individual schools and so undermines one of the key responsibilities of LEAs under the 1981 Act. This will become more evident in future with the reduced capability of LEAs to promote further special provision in ordinary schools. Now that LMS will soon apply to special schools, LEAs will be able to decide how many places they will provide in the different special educational needs areas. But, they will not have much influence without clear legislative backing, which does not exist despite vague general commitments, to promote integration in ordinary schools. This outcome reflects the Government's past reluctance to support the LEAs in taking an active role in protecting and promoting the interests of all children in the locality, especially the more vulnerable children, such as children with special educational needs. There is little indication in the White Paper that there will be any change in regard to promoting integration organisationally within ordinary schools.

The conclusion to this background section is that the 1981 and 1988 Acts are not in principle incompatible. The principles underlying the National Curriculum and LMS are compatible with common curriculum entitlements for all and with greater integration in ordinary schools. Where the 1988 Act works against the 1981 Act is in the specific form of a national curriculum and school autonomy which has been adopted. In excluding some explicit school influence on the form and practice of the National Curriculum, and in reducing LEA capability to fulfil their responsibilities to provide for children with special educational needs in integrated settings, the 1988 Act undermines the basis of the 1981 Act.

Individual *v.* regulated market approach

The basic flaw in the 1988 Act derives from the excessive reliance on individualistic parental choice as the means of regulating an effective education system for all. It is a flaw from many perspectives and not just in relation to special educational needs. A more satisfactory principle would recognise the balancing of individual choice with the need to protect the choices of all individuals, especially those from vulnerable and disadvantaged minorities. This would require a local agency representing the wider local interests, whether an LEA or some regionally based authority, such as the proposed Funding Agency, with powers and responsibilities to act in the wider interest. The implication of this position for the 1988 Act is that the principles of a common curriculum and local school management need to be preserved, while the National Curriculum and LMS are redesigned to restore a local regulative aspect to their form and operation.

The White Paper proposals for developing a system of independently managed grant maintained schools (GMS), with the new system of school inspection, goes even further to undo the current local authority base of school provision and its regulation. There are at this stage many uncertainties about the GMS proposals, but a gradual transfer is envisaged of LEA responsibilities to the proposed FAS for securing sufficient and suitable places. For the wider groups of those with special educational needs (without Statements), there will be shared LEA/FAS responsibilities and eventual full FAS responsibility. For those with Statements the Government envisages that the LEA and FAS will share responsibilities. These arrangements for shared responsibilities could lead to a less coherent and effective system of overseeing special education provision in a locality.

One of the fears about GMS has been that the schools would be reluctant to provide fully for the range of special educational needs. It is thought that this will result from increased competition for places, informal entry requirements and moves to formal changes in the character of the schools, despite the responsibilities of their governing bodies to secure appropriate provision for those with special educational needs. Some evidence from six grant maintained schools has suggested that heads do not consider that more competition would make any difference to their willingness to accept those with severe special educational needs (Audit Commission/HMI, 1992). It needs to be noted that grant maintained schools are few and may be keen to prove themselves at this stage especially in this area. If more schools become grant maintained, attitudes to accepting and genuinely providing appropriate provision for those with special educational needs may crystallise as less favourable. However, to counter this, the Government plans to give parents the right to state their preference of school, including grant maintained schools. Whether such rights, even with the right to appeal and tribunal decisions binding on the LEAs, will be realised in practice will be discussed in what follows. But what is clear is that any changes to the 1981 Act need to be seen in the wider context of operation of the 1988 Act and the proposals set out in the White Paper (DES, 1992b).

THE SIGNIFICANCE OF THE 1981 ACT

Positive aspects

The 1981 Act has been widely acclaimed by many educationalists as a progressive and enlightened piece of legislation which has established the field of special educational needs as an important aspect of education. There are several variations on this theme. Progress has been attributed to the 'abandoning of handicap categories', the adoption of the principle of integration and the increased participation of parents in decisions about their children's needs and provision. I prefer to focus on the variation which emphasises that the 1981 Act was pro-integration in principle, rather than the one which celebrates the abandoning of categories. The 1981 Act placed the duty on LEAs to educate children with special educational needs in ordinary schools. Although general limiting conditions for integration were specified and no significant Government funds were available, the principle was embodied in law.

It is often not recognised how the integration principle is closely connected with the introduction of the concept of special educational needs. The concept of special educational needs was introduced to cover both children in special schools and those with difficulties in ordinary schools. By assuming that no clear dividing line could be drawn between the 'handicapped' and the 'non-handicapped' the intention was to highlight what was in common between all pupils. This is an expression of the principle of integration and a way of recognising that all children can learn with appropriate opportunities and provision. The introduction of the special educational needs concept was, therefore, not just a way of promoting the education of children with impairments and disabilities in ordinary schools, but also a way of formally recognising the wider group of children with difficulties, who need appropriate learning opportunities. The concept of special educational needs is an integral concept in that it links those previously in special schools with those who were always in ordinary schools. These positive aspects of the 1981 Act still deserve support.

Another positive aspect of the 1981 Act, as mentioned above, was the recognition of parental rights to request assessment and take part in statutory assessment and decisions about provision. This represented a significant move towards legally recognising the crucial role of parents in the education of their children with special educational needs. It redressed some of the imbalance between the professionals and parents, even though there was much still to be done. Parents have had rights to appeal under the 1981 Act, and to make formal complaints under the 1944 Act, if they do not agree with LEA decisions. However, if local tribunals have supported a parental position, LEAs have not been bound by the tribunal decision.

It is interesting that the Audit Commission/HMI report (1992) has argued recently for giving parents of those with Statements the same rights to state their preferences for a school as parents of other pupils, something which they have not had under the 1981 Act. In the recent consultation paper about amending the 1981 Act (DFE, 1992a), the Government is proposing, as mentioned above, to extend to parents of children with Statements of special educational needs the same right to state a preference for their child's school as other parents. The LEA would be required to comply with this preference provided certain conditions were met. Linked to this is the further proposal that parents would have the right to appeal in connection with the school mentioned in a Statement. These proposals are in principle of considerable significance for educating those with special educational needs in ordinary schools and deserve to be strongly supported.

Negative aspects

Alongside these positive aspects are negative features which I will discuss in turn with suggestions for changes to the legislation. I will focus on three negative aspects:

1. the definition of special educational needs;

2. the use of the statutory assessment and issuing Statements of special educational needs;

3. duties on LEAs and schools and their lack of specificity in the present circumstances.

This analysis will not cover in detail all relevant aspects of the 1981 Act. As regards the age range which it covers, all that needs to be said here is that it is time to extend a clear unconditional duty on LEAs in the Act to young people over the age 16 with special educational needs. Although there is some uncertainty about how this would work in the context of the changes to the further education system, the principle needs to be recognised in the Act. As regards what counts as special educational provision, there has been some clarification of when speech therapy is special educational provision, following the 1989 Lancashire case, which has been included in some alterations to the Circular 22/89 on the workings of the 1981 Act (DES, 1989a). Perhaps this clarification would be best incorporated into new regulations in a way which applied the principle that where the need for any therapy was educational it would count as special educational need. My intention, however, is rather to concentrate more on the negative aspects of the 1981 Act which relate to underlying principles and changing circumstances.

The definition of special educational needs

Starting with the concept of special educational needs in the 1981 Act, it can be argued that one of the main problems derives from a confusion in the Warnock report itself about the coverage of special education. Paragraph 3.38 (page 46) of the Warnock report states that special education:

> encompasses the whole range and variety of additional help, wherever it is provided and whether on a full or part time basis, by which children may

be helped to overcome educational difficulties, however they are caused. (DES, 1978, para 3.38)

This is an over-inclusive view, which was recognised in the formulation of the 1981 Act itself, when difficulties arising when the difference of the home from the teaching language were excluded from the definition of learning difficulties. There was also no mention of high abilities as requiring additional help. I mention this point mainly to illustrate how the Warnock concept of special educational needs clearly implies disability and impairment, while wishing to abandon it.

There was also, and continues to be, a confusion about the term 'learning difficulties', as to whether it refers to problems in school learning arising from different kinds of impairments and conditions, or whether it specifically refers to intellectual or cognitive difficulties. There is a need to clarify the meaning of the term 'learning difficulties', and for this reason I will talk of difficulties of learning, in this pamphlet, with the assumption that they can arise from child and environmental factors.

Several influential commentators have also stressed that the then 'new' concept of special educational needs was circular and relative to individual circumstances of provision. This circularity is supposed to be shown in the following excerpts:

a child has special educational needs if he has a learning difficulty which calls for special educational provision [section 1(1)] and
a child has a learning difficulty if he has a significantly greater difficulty in learning than the majority of the children of his age. [section 1(2a)]

These two excerpts only show a circularity if something like this third statement, which is not in the Act, is added:

A child who has a significantly greater difficulty in learning has special educational needs.

In fact a careful reading of the wording shows that the 1981 Act definitions makes an explicit reference to disability. This is shown in section 1(2b) of the Act:

2 ...a child has learning difficulties if a. he has a *significantly greater difficulty in learning* than the majority of children of his age; OR b. he has a *disability*

which either prevents or hinders him from making use of educational facilities of a kind generally provided in schools, within the area of the local authority. (my italic)

It is more accurate to describe the 1981 Act definitions as over-general and lacking in clear and specific definitions of what are significant difficulties. Any implied circularity would then be opened up.

Relative and interactionist definitions

This definition has also been welcomed for being relative in the sense that a child's special educational needs are identified in relationship to the educational situations in which she or he is expected to function. This has been interpreted as implying that :

i. the better a school is at meeting the range of individual differences, the smaller will be the number of those with special educational needs; and
ii. the better a school is at meeting the range of special educational needs through its own arrangements and its use of generally available support services, then fewer children will be subject to Statements. (Select Committee 1987)

It is relevant to the question of relativity that the House of Commons Select Committee on special educational needs reported that their evidence suggested that the relativity of definition caused uncertainty and confusion. This evidence reflects widespread views about the lack of clarity about when a pupil has special educational needs. That special educational needs are relative has been supported in terms of two positions, mentioned in a previous section:

i. that no clear distinction can be drawn between those who are handicapped and those who are not;
ii. that environmental factors including school ones can cause and aggravate learning difficulties.

The first position is usually seen as contrary to the view that there is an absolute and definitive division between normality and handicap. The second position is usually seen as opposed to what is called the deficit model. This is the assumption that pupils' difficulties arise only from their own internal deficiencies.

My contention is that part of the problem with the definition of special educational needs in the 1981 Act is an uncritical perspective on relative definitions. It is possible to agree with a position which recognises:

* a continuum between normality and disability,
* an interaction between child and environmental causes of learning difficulties and
* practical difficulties with current definitions of special educational needs.

For this argument, I propose that we think of special educational needs as being concerned with that additional or different provision, which enables a child with difficulties of learning, whose current level is significantly below some standard or norm, to make progress in learning. For this purpose it is not necessary to specify the kinds of learning difficulties or their origins.

This working definition implies that performance is assessed informally and perhaps intuitively against some norm of satisfactory progress. We would also expect norms of progress and attainment to differ between teachers within schools, between schools within LEAs and between LEAs. What is important to realise is that there are norms that vary, and that this variation leads us to consider whether we wish norms to change. Though there are likely to be limits to how much norms can be altered, the critical point is that they can be altered to some extent. They are not facts of nature. This means, for example, that individuals or organisations may want to raise the level of satisfactory educational progress for all or some children. The Education Reform Act 1988 is an example of a Government trying to do this. But others, whether individuals, schools or LEAs, may also wish to alter their own norms in their own ways. The setting of norms can therefore be done at national or more local levels. Norms of educational progress can also be set more loosely or tightly. Introducing the National Curriculum is an example of the Government establishing fairly tight national norms to apply to all children.

When a Government sets norms of educational progress this involves exercising its political power. When LEAs set cut off points or thresholds, whether loose or tight, for providing additional resources for some children this also involves an exercise of power. In view of the scarcity of educational funds, LEAs have no option but to exercise their power to make a distinction between those who will get additional resources and those who will not. This is where there is a basic confusion in the view that no clear distinction can be drawn between those with and those without special educational needs. There is no absolute distinction between those with and those without special educational needs because the cut-off line will depend partly on the availability of additional resources. In view of this, and because difficulties of learning are a matter of degree, there is no simple way of setting a cut-off line. But this does not mean that the setting of criteria for allocating additional resources can or should be avoided.

It follows from this that special educational needs and difficulties of learning are relative in the sense that they are assessed partly in terms of norms of satisfactory attainment levels and rates of progress. However, relativity in this sense does not require abandoning criteria for deciding who is eligible for additional resources. I want to propose, therefore, that we need to clarify, as far as possible, what kinds and degrees of pupils' difficulties of learning in what circumstances of teaching are entitled to what kinds of additional provision. To be clear, we need to define or categorise these kinds of special educational provision which apply to children in general terms. This position is supported by the Audit Commission/HMI report (1992) on special educational provision which identifies the lack of clarity about what constitutes special educational needs as a major problem underlying several of the difficulties in implementing the 1981 Act.

Kinds of definitions

We also need to distinguish between *definitions of special educational need and provision* and *definitions of difficulties of learning*. Definitions of special educational need are linked to definitions of provision, since what is needed, in the end, is provision. These definitions would identify those kinds of special educational methods and approaches required to meet educational goals. It is sometimes thought that there are special approaches only for needs based on physical difficulties, such as sensory or motor difficulties, and not for mild intellectual or emotional or behaviour difficulties. It is useful in defining special educational approaches to assume a gradation of approaches from those similar to general ones to those which are very distinct from general ones. The position taken in this pamphlet is that, even if adaptations to general provision only involve lower teacher-pupil ratios then it is important to be clear at what ratio the change in general provision becomes special provision.

Definitions of difficulties of learning can be of child, home and/or school origin, of physiological and/or psychological nature, such as hearing impairment or emotional problems, and short term or long term. Those difficulties, usually physiological and long term, which are associated with medical diagnostic categories, through the historical involvement of medical doctors in special education, have often led to a confusion between educational and medical definitions of difficulties (Norwich, 1990). Kinds of difficulties of learning are concerned with educational goals and methods; medical categories of illness, disorder or impairment are concerned with therapeutic goals and treatments. Though separate, these systems are related. Medical categories are sometimes relevant to assessing difficulties of learning, when, for example, an organic difficulty is not treatable and likely to be long term. In such circumstances knowing the implications of an impairment has relevance in the wider context of other learner and environmental strengths and weaknesses. Arguments for abandoning conceptions or categories of difficulties of learning or special educational needs and provision are, therefore, misguided and have interfered with the effective provision for children with special educational needs (Warnock, 1991).

It is important also in this context to note that this position is fully compatible with an approach which sees difficulties of learning as having both environmental and child causes. In this context it has been argued that there is a compensatory interaction between child and environmental strengths and weaknesses (Wedell, 1983). Personal and environmental strengths can compensate for weaknesses, but recognising this does not imply that compensatory interaction can overcome or remedy the difficulties and result in normal rates and levels of learning. This point is relevant to the view that the 1981 Act is based on an interactionist view about the origins of difficulties in learning. However, what this means has not been made clear as regards the assessment of difficulties of learning. Clarification requires that neither child nor environmental factors be excluded from assessment.

This means, in practice, that the assessment of difficulties will focus on the child's strengths and weaknesses, the environment's strengths and weaknesses and their interaction. The practical implications of this have not been fully worked out in the assessment system under the 1981 Act, despite the interactionist rhetoric. Professional advisers to LEAs, if they were acting according to this model, would be involved in assessing both the strengths and weaknesses of the child *and* the child's learning opportunities, experiences and activities in school. As these advisers use criteria to decide on the significance and degree of child causal factors, so they would use criteria about the significance and degree of factors associated with learning opportunities. For example, consider the situation in which a child's learning difficulties can be largely attributed to a lack of good enough teaching, which an ordinary school could be expected to provide. This would have to be based on assessments of learning opportunities using criteria about good enough teaching. How such assessments are best done has not been fully worked out since the 1981 Act has come into operation.

The need for definitions

The need for general definitions or categories of provision derives from a principle of fairness—that children with similar difficulties in similar school circumstances in different parts of the area and country receive comparable provision. It is important to be clear about this. There is no suggestion that there are absolute definitions about inherent, innate or fixed child characteristics. The argument for greater clarity and specificity of definitions is one for fair decisions about educational provision. A view consistent with this position was expressed by the House of Commons Select Committee (1987) which said:

> There is a strong case for more guidance about identifying the wider range of special educational needs and about when a Statement of need might be required (para.26) and
> There is uncertainty about what constitutes special education provision. We recommend that national guidance on such provision should be given. (para.27)

This position is further supported by the recent Audit Commission/HMI report (1992), which recommends that there be national guidelines on the threshold for statutory assessment and a linked framework for defining responsibilities of ordinary schools for special educational needs. The Government appears to now recognise the need for such guidance in its recent consultation paper on amending the 1981 Act (DFE, 1992a).

Providing such guidance will require differentiating between the kinds of special education provision, something which we already do, and was in fact advised by the Warnock Report. Nevertheless, the make-believe that categories have been abandoned still persists in some quarters. In short, what is needed are educationally relevant, specific and non-pejorative definitions and criteria to act as rules for deciding eligibility for additional resources. Setting these definitions could but does not have to be done at a national level. We could envisage Government requiring LEAs or some other regional authorities to develop specific definitions within a general national framework—a *national framework with a requirement for local definition*. These proposals, to repeat the points above, are compatible with an interactionist causal view about the origins of difficulties of learning. They also acknowledge the relativity of special educational needs, but in a way which recognises the need for general categories or definitions for additional resource allocation.

One possible reason for the force behind the position that we abandon categories is the aim to abandon stigmatising and devaluing attitudes and practices, as part of an integrationist philosophy. If so, it is important to realise this, as it is an aim deserving strong support. In doing so, we could ask whether abandoning categories of special provision will lead to a reduction of stigma and devaluation. The position taken here is that changes in the social esteem and material position of those with special needs are a more significant means of reducing devaluation than abandoning labels. By answering in this way we would distinguish between abandoning definitions of additional provision eligibility—something which has not happened—and altering the negative processes of categorising to exclude and stigmatise children (Pumfrey and Mittler, 1989). The 1981 Act has made a significant first step to this end, but the aim of reducing categorising and stigmatising might be aided by abandoning the statutory assessment Statementing procedures themselves. This will be discussed below.

Difficulties in developing definitions

The definition of special educational needs in the 1981 Act ultimately depends on the definition of what it means for the 'LEA to determine special educational provision'. Section 7.1 of the Act states:

> the LEA shall...if they are of the opinion that they should determine the special education provision that should be made for him [the child], make a Statement of special educational needs. (1981 Act, section 7(1))

Cox (1981), a lawyer who has written about the 1981 Act, explains that the meaning of this depends on making reference to circulars, though circulars do not have the legal force of Act and regulations. But even the circulars do not give us much clarity on the matter. I will try to summarise the circular guidance for when the LEA is to determine provision.

Circular 8/81 (DES, 1981), concerned with transitional arrangements for introducing the 1981 Act, identified three conditions for when children should have Statements:

a.   all children then in special schools;
b.   when extra resources (staff + equipment) are required to cater for special educational needs in ordinary schools;
c.   those ascertained as handicapped under the 1944 Act.

Circular 1/83 (DES, 1983) explained that Statements are required for:

a.   children with severe and complex learning difficulties which require extra resources in ordinary schools;
b.   those in special schools and units. (para.14)

Statements were not required when:

the ordinary school provides special education provision from its own resources e.g. additional tuition, attending reading centre or unit for disruption. (para.15)

The most recent Circular, 22/89 (DES, 1989a), is even less clear, giving the conditions only when Statements are not required:

a.   when the ordinary school determines and makes special educational provision;
b.   when attendance is at a tuition centre;
c.   short term or part time provision;
d.   temporary placement in special school or unit with parents' agreement.

The DES in this circular explain their reluctance to clarify matters in the following terms:

It is not possible to prescribe precise limits for this smaller group. (ibid. para. 29)

The reason given is that:

The factors which will influence the LEA's decision whether or not they should determine the special education provision for an individual child will vary from area to area depending on how the LEA aims to meet special educational needs. (ibid.)

This statement begs the question of whether it is acceptable for LEAs to organise special educational provision outside a clear national framework and how the DES itself aimed to influence the way LEAs meet special educational needs. It seems that the DES was in the grip of the misconceptions discussed above. Reference to the relativity of special educational needs should not excuse central government from establishing a clear national special education framework. As argued above, it is a false choice to pose an absolutist versus a relativist approach to special educational needs as alternatives. There is a third way which seeks to establish a framework for developing specific and reviewable general definitions to be used for making decisions about providing additional resources. This is a question of fairness, effectiveness and consistency.

The Audit Commission/HMI report recognised the practical difficulties in developing specific definitions, but made no comments on the philosophical reservations about categories associated with a prevalent interpretation of the 1981 Act. It is not possible here to present definitions in concrete detail, but there are several procedural principles which could be followed. A national framework for definitions and local formulations of specific pilot definitions could be drawn up by working groups at national and local levels involving professionals, administrators and parents. These could be trialled and reformulated before adoption, within a system of review and development underpinned by Regulation. In establishing definitions, positions would have to be taken on questions like these:

a. What kinds of difficulties of learning are there?
b. What can be achieved with children with different kinds and degrees of difficulties of learning given certain kinds of provision?
c. What kinds of special provision are there?

d. What are the purposes of the definitions and the feasibility of these purposes—eligibility for special provision and/or prescriptions for special education provision for individual pupils?

e. At what level of generality will a national framework be formulated and what would its relationship be to how much variation of definitions there will be at local level?

f. Will assessment techniques be prescribed at local level or decisions be left to individual professionals or services?

There is no doubt that such definitions if they are to prove useful in practice would involve complex criteria and indicators which would require setting thresholds along scales or dimensions, such as reading accuracy. This movement towards clarifying the groups of pupils with special educational needs will involve a basic challenge to current conceptions about the nature and purposes of identifying those with special educational needs. It would involve a change to the basic formulation of definitional terms in the 1981 Act.

The use of the statutory assessment and having Statements of special educational needs

Administrative difficulties

I will now turn to the second negative aspect of the 1981 Act—the system of statutory assessment for some children with special educational needs and having Statements of special educational needs. The case against the assessment procedures and Statementing are partly to do with their purposes and partly to do with means. Some criticism has been levelled against the relatively high staffing requirements of have statutory assessment, given the limited resources available. There has also been considerable concern expressed over how long the procedures take, over the quality and specificity of the final statements, their usefulness to new teachers who become involved with the children and whether LEAs even inform parents fully of their rights. These problems were fully illustrated in 1988 evaluation study done at the London University Institute of Education of the workings of the 1981 Act (Goacher *et al.*, 1988). They are even more strongly highlighted by the findings of the Audit Commission /HMI report (1992).

There is obviously scope for improvements in these matters—time deadlines could be introduced, Statement writers and professional advisers could have more training, LEAs could publish performance criteria for administering Statements, there could be more accountability and inspection of an LEA's implementation of the 1981 Act assessment procedures, and so on. Circular 22/89 and the recent additions to it are recommending greater specificity in the formulations of special educational needs (DES, 1989a). The Audit Commission/HMI report (1992) is recommending a new type of Statement which includes specific objectives and the resources in cash terms. In the new consultation paper on the 1981 Act (DFE, 1992) the Government proposes to legislate to ensure that statutory assessment and Statementing procedures are done within specific timescales. This proposal is to be welcomed.

The function of statutory assessment

However, in connection with the usefulness of Statements to new teachers (of children with Statements), it has been argued (Wedell, 1991) that the purpose of statutory assessment is mainly for the LEA to decide and justify the allocation of additional resources. The purpose is to decide on eligibility, not to provide specific assessment information for specific teaching purposes. If this is so, then one cannot expect to meet these differing assessment purposes with the same assessment methods. Accordingly, summative statutory assessment procedures cannot easily provide the kinds of assessments required for developing specific teaching programmes. Summative statutory assessments can be used, however, as the starting points for more specific and further curriculum related assessment. These points argue against the Audit Commission support for specific teaching objectives in favour of general objectives, to be specifying by those about to teach the children with Statements. However, this position is compatible with specific details about resources to be included in Statements.

Related to these assessments of special educational needs is the way in which the Statement information is used for the planning of teaching and for the annual review. The 1981 Act requires annual reviews of special educational needs, but there is little central guidance about the exact form this would take. The Audit Commission/HMI report (1992) make much of the weaknesses of the annual review process and sees it as a major way of ensuring accountability for LEA special educational provision. If a review is to enable a considered reassessment of needs, this is best done in the context of fairly specific educational goals and methods. These would be best formulated at the start of the LEA determined special provision, whether in special schools, units or mainstream placements. This calls for a system of specific planning of teaching for the pupil, which is of particular importance for mainstream placements as there is a need to plan how the educational goals and methods for the child can be coordinated with the provision for other children in the mainstream class. It would involve coordinated planning by the class teacher and support teachers, whether from a LEA peripatetic service or an outreach from special school.

Unless there is such a system, there is no way to ensure that the child will receive the education s/he needs, which under the 1981 Act is one condition relevant to the duty of educating children with special educational needs in ordinary schools. This calls, therefore, for an additional requirement to the 1981 Act, perhaps in the form of Regulations, that LEAs ensure that those responsible for LEA determined provision make use of the previous assessments about the pupil as the basis for comprehensive and detailed planning and reviewing of teaching. One of the advantages of specific planning systems for individuals is that in acting as the basis for annual reviews of learning progress, they could provide evaluative feedback about the summative assessments which led to the LEA determining special provision.

Conceptual confusion

While discussing the form and functions of Statements, it is appropriate to comment on a conceptual confusion about the nature of special educational needs and special educational provision. Government guidance about the format of Statements and what to include under each section does not recognise the logical connection between needs and provision (Norwich, 1990). When a child is said to have a need this includes three elements:

* an educational norm or goal, the ends;
* a significant gap between the child's current functioning and the goal;
* the needed learning provision, the means, that will enable the child to reach the goal.

The concept of 'need' is complex because it refers, not just to the child's functioning and the educational intentions for the child, but to the provision or conditions to fulfil these intentions. This is the reason that the 'need' concept has been seen as more positive than one like 'educational handicap', which refers only to gaps or deficits. As I have said, advice about a child's special educational needs will include advice about relevant provision. An LEA may or may not be able to make this needed provision available for the child. When it cannot, then there is a difference between *optimum provision and available provision*. This distinction has typically not been made in the operation of the 1981 Act. The tension between the ideal and real has usually been seen to be between needs and provision. The effect of this has been to weaken the detailed and specific formulation of needs in terms of optimum, or even good enough, provision.

This issue relates to the major concern which has come to media attention recently in the context of LEA financial cut backs, that professional advice is too strongly influenced by available provision. This involves defining individual children's needs to fit what provision is available, rather than make the needed optimum or even good enough provision available. It has been argued that the statutory procedures at least enable parents to influence the process of defining and determining their children's special educational needs. It is true that this has provided some check on LEAs fulfilling their duties to make provision on the basis of at least parents' views of need. However, this is a very expensive, and at times a distressing and time consuming way of matching provision to need. I will return to this point shortly.

Purposes of Statementing

I want to turn now to the criticisms of the purposes of statutory assessment and having Statements. The Warnock Report argued against categories mainly because they were seen to be part of a stigmatising and devaluing process of labelling. The 1981 Act accepted the then 'new' concept of special educational needs, but went on to adopt a statutory LEA labelling procedure, without recognising any tension. The value of the Statement is seen as providing some security or protection for the child with special educational needs. However, phrases like 'the protection of the Statement' cannot be taken at face validity for several reasons:

  i. In many LEAs additional resources have been allocated to individual children or individual children placed in special schools or units without their undergoing statutory assessment;
  ii. LEAs have been often reluctant and/or unable financially to provide the advised provision and have therefore not issued a Statement;

iii. In some LEAs children have been issued Statements without any additional resources.

What we seem to have had is an inefficient system of labelling children supposedly to justify and earmark additional resources for them. It would be possible to improve the assessment system to become more efficient and effective. This is the line taken by the Audit Commission/HMI report (1992) and is proposed by the Government in the new consultation document (DFE,1992a). Were this to happen, labelling might be acceptable as a legitimate disadvantage when balanced against the greater benefit of securing and protecting additional resources. However, it is often hard to take this trade off seriously in the current climate of change in the schools and LEAs and the insufficiencies in school funding. In this context, there are also two crucial questions which have to be considered:

1. Is identifying individual children the only way for LEAs to allocate additional resources to them?
2. Is a system of statutory assessment and maintaining Statements the best or only way of protecting these additional resources?

Alternate forms of resource allocation

Dessent (1987) in addressing the first question, has answered clearly and persuasively that there are other ways of allocating additional resources. The principle is to allocate these additional resources to individual ordinary schools in proportion to their requirements for children with special educational needs. This scheme of resource allocation can be seen as a way of providing for more children with severe difficulties in ordinary schools. It would also reduce the stigmatising effects of statutory individual assessment. It is acknowledged, as I understand this view, that there would still be some resource allocation made through statutory procedures for individual assessment. In practice, the local management of schools system of funding does now enable the meeting of individual special educational needs through such an arrangement. But, it does involve having to establish procedures for assessing individual schools' needs for additional resources. This will inevitably require a set of general definitions and criteria relating in part to the range, type and number of children with special educational needs. So, even if additional resourcing for children with special educational needs is via ordinary schools, there will be a need for specific and clear general definitions and criteria. This takes us back to the earlier problems of the role of general definitions in resource allocation. It is interesting that the Select Committee supported a system of school allocation as a way of reducing the pressures on LEAs to carry out statutory assessments and make Statements (Select Committee Report, 1987, para.33). The Audit Commission/HMI report (1992) has also underlined the importance of a comprehensive strategy to increase the capability of ordinary schools as a way of reducing the demand and number of issued Statements.

The recent pressures on LEAs to undertake statutory assessments arise from concerns about the future availability of additional resources without Statements and from pressures on schools arising from implementing the Education Reform Act changes. The systematic cut back in local government spending on education is also very significant. So, although allocating additional special educational resources through the LMS scheme could reduce the incidence of statutory assessment over time, this depends critically on how much is in fact allocated overall to special education and to ordinary schools.

Protecting additional resources

This brings me to the second of the two above questions: Is a system of statutory assessment and maintaining Statements the only way of protecting these resources? It has been noted that the 1981 Act embodies resource allocation principles which belonged to an era when special education was more strictly identified with special schooling. However, now that special education involves provision for children with significant difficulties both in ordinary and separate schools, it could be argued that Statements provide protection for those children receiving special provision in ordinary schools.

Given the doubts which I have raised about the administration of statutory assessment and making Statements, confidence in its future depends not just on administrative effectiveness, but whether its basic purpose can still command support. Part of the problem results from a misconception that protection derives from having a Statement. The Statement can only afford protection if the specific provision is available and parents have access to a binding appeal system about what provision is needed and whether it is made available. The erosion of confidence in the principle of the protection provided by a Statement can be attributed mainly to these two factors:

1. the decisions of tribunals adjudicating when parents contest LEA provision decisions have not been binding on LEAs;
2. the duties placed on LEAs to meet special educational needs have been insufficiently specified and inadequately monitored and inspected.

It follows that for Statements to ensure protection of provision the appeals system and the specification of the duties on LEAs need to be tightened. The Government have recently announced their plans to establish a new single tier system of regional tribunals with the power to make their decisions binding on LEAs (DFE, 1992a). The idea is to have tribunals which are more independent and whose decisions are binding on all parties. Part of these proposals is to widen the parents' rights to include, for example, appeals against an LEA's refusal to make an assessment or re-assessment and an LEA decision to cease to maintain a Statement. These proposals deserve to be welcomed in principle, even if it brings parents and LEAs occasionally into disagreements. It would also be appropriate to involve pupils' views about placement decisions, when pupils are able to give a considered opinion. Doing this might help to resolve disagreements between LEAs and parents if they occur.

Ensuring the protection of provision for pupils with special educational needs, would also depend on a thorough inspection of LEA determined special education provision, perhaps by the new OFSTED or some other agency like the Audit Commission. The Audit Commission/HMI report (1992) has also outlined ways in which LEAs could be given incentives to implement fully the 1981 Act. Finding more effective ways of holding LEAs more accountable for special education provision is an important step in rebuilding confidence in the protection of the statement of special educational needs.

The statutory basis for protecting special education provision is in the relevant sections of the 1944 and 1981 Education Acts:

1944 Act, 8 . 2 (c):

In fulfilling their duties under this section a local education authority shall in particular, have regard to c. to the need for securing that special educational provision is made for pupils with special educational needs.

1981 Act

Section 2—duties on LEAs:
2[1] to secure provision;
2[2] to educate in ordinary school;
2[3] conditions to take into account;
2[4] to review arrangements.

Section 2—duties on school governors:
2[5] a. to make best endeavour to secure special educational provision;
 b. to make needs known to teachers;
 c. to secure that teachers are aware of importance of assessing and providing;
2[7] to secure that the child with special educational needs engages in school activities with others.

I am proposing that these duties provide the starting points for developing a more genuine protection of special education provision. How these duties can be specified and elaborated is discussed in the next section. If and when a more genuine protection of special educational provision is established, it will no longer be necessary for all children currently with Statements to undergo the full statutory assessment procedures and have a Statement. A change to the system of statutory assessment and having Statements is proposed only as part of wider changes to establish a more genuine protection of special educational provision.

What I am not proposing, however, is the complete abandonment of the system of statutory assessment and Statementing. There are good reasons to keep the current system for those situations in which parents *wish* to have their children undergo this procedure. They may use this right when they wish to appeal against the type and amount of additional provision which the LEA and the school offer. Hopefully, the effect of this would be to remove many pupils from the time consuming statutory assessment procedures. Most pupils would receive additional or different provision based on assessments and decisions made more rapidly and without procedural formalities.

Brahm Norwich

Parental option for full statutory assessments

Introducing a parental option for the statutory assessment procedures and having Statements would itself require some changes to the 1981 Act. This would have to cover both circumstances; when parents *did not opt* for statutory procedures and when they *did opt*. Parents could opt for the full statutory assessment procedures when they wished to contest or clarify some aspect of the Statement and the provision made available. This option would require a development of the existing 1981 Act system, as the outcome of a parental appeal would be binding on the LEA, subject to further appeal. Without this development, parental rights could not be regarded as meaningful.

When parents do not opt for the full statutory assessment procedures, they would be choosing the more streamlined and flexible LEA decision making procedures for pupils receiving LEA determined special education provision—to be called, for simplicity, the *required assessment*. How this option for the required assessment would operate would need to be specified in legislation. In such Regulations parents would still have rights to influence assessment and the specification of need and provision. LEAs would still be required to assess special educational needs. There would still be professional assessments, with the requirement that there be at least one internal assessment, by the teacher of the child, and at least one external assessment, by a professional who is independent of the school. However, there would be no wait periods before proceeding with assessments and less formal communications, as there are under the present procedures. There could also be some flexibility over whether educational, psychological and medical assessments are always required. In some circumstances the LEA could decide to involve only a minimum of professional advisers, such as an educational psychologist, and a teacher assessment from the professional side. This could be done rapidly by an LEA panel consisting of senior professionals and administrators, including an educational adviser, a psychologist and a medical officer, to make decisions about the minimum professional assessment advice required in particular cases. Medical advice would sometimes, but not always, be required, unlike at present.

The system of *required assessment* would enable LEAs to operate a more flexible and rapid system of decision making about whether to determine the special educational provision. If, following the required assessment, the LEA decided to determine the provision for a particular pupil, then there would still be a duty on the LEA to record the special educational provision, appropriate school and other arrangements and additional non-educational provision (i.e. only sections 3, 4 and 5 of the Statement as it is). Such a *record* of special educational provision could be linked to the duty to make this available, as at present. But LEAs would not make a full Statement including a description of the child's functioning and special educational needs, nor would the relevant professional advice be included. These aspects of the full statutory assessment and Statementing system would be available to parents, but not be part of the required assessment and record of special education provision option.

It is important to be clear about the differences between the proposed *required assessment* and the *full statutory assessment* options. The required assessment system would involve fewer and less formal communications with parents, reduce the waiting periods before proceeding with next stages and involve fewer professional advisers than the full statutory assessment under the 1981 Act. The LEA's decision to determine the special educational provision would be simply in the form of a short *record*, compared with fuller and more complex *Statement*. Yet, parental opting for the shorter system would not affect the duty on LEAs to secure the provision which the LEA decides is needed. But, with the shorter system, there would be no right of appeal against the LEA decisions. If parents wanted that, then they could opt for the full system of statutory assessment with Statementing, as the basis for pursuing an appeal. They could opt for this either as an option at the stage that it seemed likely that their child's needs could not be met out of generally available provision, or even after going through the shorter system of assessment. The intention behind proposing this dual system of assessment and decision making is, 1. to enable more efficient decision making when there is agreement between the parties involved and 2. to retain and enhance a system for adjudicating when there are disagreements. It is interesting that although the Audit Commission/HMI report (1992) believes that Statements can issued in well under six months under the current full procedures, it does still mention briefly the prospect of a shortened procedure.

Duties to provide special education provision

This brings me to the third and last negative aspect of the 1981 Act—attributing duties and their lack of specificity in the present circumstances. There have been considerable concerns, as mentioned above, about the negative effects of the 1988 Education Reform Act on the developments and provision associated with the

1981 Act. I do not intend to explore these at any length, other than relate the effects to four of the key relevant features of this legislation:

1. open enrolment in schools;
2. the National Curriculum;
3. local management of schools;
4. grant maintained schools.

As discussed above, these changes are meant to promote more competition between schools for children, with parents choosing between schools. 'Market' choice is supposed to be based on information about children's attainments and the school's profile of attainments arrived at through the National Curriculum assessment arrangements. The likely effect is to make ordinary schools, which are now responsible for allocating their budgets, to be more aware of the resource needs of children with special educational needs. The immediate effect has been an increasing demand for statutory assessment and the resulting pressure on special resources. Concerns have also centred on the effect of the requirements to delegate a larger proportion of funds to schools. In the context of more schools becoming grant maintained in the wake of the White Paper, this leaves the LEAs with decreasing influence to carry out their special education duties in both authority and grant maintained schools.

The Audit Commission/HMI report (1992) identified a reluctance of LEAs to delegate resources currently used for central support teams to schools. A lack of accountability by schools to LEAs was one of the major weaknesses identified in this report. In recommending that funds for support in ordinary schools be delegated to the schools the report advised LEAs to develop mechanisms to hold schools accountable. The problem with this recommendation, one of the key ones in the Audit Commission report, is the assumption that increased accountability can be introduced without being reinforced by legislative changes.

The formulation of the 1981 Act is no longer relevant in the current circumstances. The devolution of powers to school governors has been seen as limiting the role of LEAs, and now with the White Paper proposals the Government envisages the eventual transfer of responsibilities to the proposed Funding Agency. The devolution of powers through LMS, the growth of grant maintained schools and the prospect of LEAs sharing responsibilities with a Funding Agency, as the number of GMS schools goes above the 10 per cent level, threatens the developing pattern of providing for pupils with special educational needs in ordinary schools. Of course, the future of LEAs depends critically on how many schools become grant maintained and, assuming that at least in some areas many more do, then this raises serious questions about the local strategic management of special education provision. It is important that those interested in special educational needs come up with relevant suggestions to best protect provision in these future circumstances.

One of the central duties placed on LEAs is to provide for special educational needs in circumstances in which schools cannot be expected to do so. There is a crucial need for some cross-school agency to fulfil this function. Whatever the future relationship between LEAs and the proposed Funding Agency, meeting special educational needs requires an agency, firstly, to determine when ordinary schools can no longer meet the special needs and secondly, to secure appropriate special educational provision in ordinary and special schools to meet these needs. Even if this second condition is met through ordinary schools providing and the LEA purchasing special educational provision for pupils with Statements, ordinary schools have to be willing to admit and work with those with Statements.

Extending duties to governing bodies

The Government's proposals to give parents the right to state a preference for ordinary school placement of their children with a Statement, and with rights to binding appeal, could put LEAs in a very weak position to comply with such a preference. The consultation paper (DFE,1992a) proposes that the LEA would consult with the governing bodies of ordinary schools over this, but if schools are unwilling or unable to meet the child's special educational needs, then the parental right would be blocked. This calls for an extension of the duties placed on LEAs to school governing bodies. Such a step would mirror the extension of management and financial responsibilities and powers to school governing bodies, adding corresponding duties for special educational needs. It is a critical principle behind the changes proposed for the 1981 Act in this pamphlet, in the context of the 1988 Act and the move towards more grant maintained schools.

Some of the duties now applying to LEAs in the 1981 Act should also apply to school governing bodies. For example, section 2(1) of the Act places a duty on LEAs to secure provision, whereas the duty on governors in 2(5)a is to use their 'best endeavour'. This requirement on governing bodies should be replaced by a straight duty as in section 2(1). The following sections place duties on LEAs:

* Section 2(2) places a duty on LEAs to educate children with special educational needs in the ordinary schools.
* Section 2(3) states the conditions to satisfy for this duty: i. account taken of parent's views; ii. child receives special educational provision required; iii. provision of efficient education for children with whom child is educated; iv. efficient use of resources.
* Section 2(4) places a duty to review arrangements.

One of the main proposals in this pamphlet is that these duties should also apply to school governing bodies. Also, in line with the previous proposal for greater clarification of the 1981 Act, there would be a need for regulations to specify and circulars to guide how these duties and conditions for integration are meant to operate. Some may see this as requiring too much of schools, but as these duties are consistent with current good practice, there seems to be every reason that governing bodies exercise their powers in accordance with the principles of educating in the ordinary school. It is important to recognise that the conditions for securing education in ordinary schools can set up limits on how much integration schools could be expected to undertake in practice. This was probably the intention in the original drafting of the 1981 Act as applied to LEAs, and can, therefore, be applied to schools as well, though there would be a need to provide central guidance on how these conditions will be interpreted.

In the extension of duties proposed, further work will be required on how the duties of both schools and LEAs would be coordinated. One way of thinking about this is to consider how parents and a school might come to seek special provision for requirements which cannot be met by generally available provision. Under the proposals in this pamphlet there would be clearer and more specific criteria for when the LEA would make special provision, whether in ordinary or special schools. Parents or schools could request consideration for special provision, though parents would decide whether they wanted the full statutory version of assessment and decision making or whether they were satisfied with the streamlined version. Whichever they opted for they would be involved in decision making. But if they wished to contest the available LEA special provision and opted for the full statutory procedures and Statement, then they could appeal to a tribunal with powers to determine what LEAs provide.

If special provision is to be made available in an ordinary school, then it is for the LEA to ensure that the school complies with its duty to educate the child, subject to the additional LEA resourcing. Now, this may present no difficulties to the school, if that school is additionally resourced for significant special educational needs (i.e. LEA determined SEN). However, if any school considers that there are grounds for not being able to carry out its duties to educate in the ordinary school, then some system could be set up for an appeal against the LEA decision. It would seem fair that this appeal should be heard by an independent tribunal whose judgement would be binding on the LEA and school. This entails that LEAs, in association with their schools, would be responsible for coordinating and planning the additional resourcing of special provision in ordinary schools. Ordinary schools would have a duty to collaborate in this, but they could contest the LEAs decisions about individual children through a tribunal system. Although this brief account does not deal with all eventualities, it does illustrate how the extension of LEA duties for special education provision could be coordinated with parallel duties for schools.

It would, however, be over-optimistic to believe that, by a simple change in the integration clauses of the 1981 Act and more clarity about the conditions for educating pupils with special educational needs in ordinary schools, the pressures against integration would subside. Legislative change needs to be part of a wider Government policy and commitment which depends on clear vision, effective leadership and adequate financial backing. Tightening up systems of administration and accountability are important but not sufficient to achieve policy goals.

CONCLUDING COMMENTS

One of the main gaps in the Government's recent proposals is any detailed consideration of the definition of special educational needs discussed in this pamphlet. The definition question affects the threshold for initiating statutory assessment, criteria for issuing Statements and what special education provision will be determined by LEAs for pupils with Statements. This gap is likely to become a problem for the Government when it comes to issuing the proposed guidance on such criteria. One can also anticipate that this definition gap will become a serious problem in the wake of setting up the proposed appeals system.

Tribunals will adjudicate between parents, with their proposed new right to state a school placement preference, and LEAs unable sometimes to comply with the preference. LEA capability to comply will depend clearly on financial resources, but also on schools sharing legal responsibilities with LEAs for those with special educational needs. It is likely that the tensions between LEAs and parents will become pronounced under the proposed system of enhanced parents' rights and diminished LEA influence in ordinary schools. Litigation could be on the increase, and this is one reason that the tribunal system needs to be carefully established in terms of its powers and membership. It is also a good reason why the definitional issues need to be addressed to facilitate the appeal system.

I have discussed some of the positive and negative aspects of the 1981 Education Act, taking some account of the Audit Commission/HMI report, recent Government plans to amend the 1981 Act, and some possible implications of the new White Paper. The analysis and the suggestions for change derive partly from the experience of using the system set up over ten years ago, but also from the needs which arise in the context of the Education Reform Act 1988. Not all possible changes have been discussed, and those I have suggested could also be worked out in more detail. My hope is that this pamphlet contributes to ideas about and proposals for amending the 1981 Act in a way that places changes in a broader conceptual framework.

RECOMMENDATIONS

1. There should be a clear unconditional duty on LEAs or on some other statutory agency to provide for young people over the age 16 with special educational needs.

2. The principle should be embodied in regulations that where any therapy is required as an educational need, that therapy would count as special educational provision.

3. There is a need to reformulate the meaning of the term 'learning difficulties', as expressed in legislation.

4. There is a need to clarify, as far as possible, what kinds and degrees of pupils' difficulties of learning in what circumstances of teaching are entitled to what kinds of additional provision. This implies the need to define or categorise as clearly as possible those kinds of special educational provision in general terms. Government could require LEAs to develop specific definitions within a general national framework – a *system of national requirement for local definition*.

5. There is a need to distinguish between *definitions of special educational need and provision* and *definitions of difficulties of learning*, whether of child, home and/or school origin, whether physiological or psychological, and whether short or long term.

6. There is a need for an additional requirement to the 1981 Act, perhaps in the form of Regulations, that LEAs ensure that those who are responsible for LEA determined provision use the previous assessments about the pupil as the basis for comprehensive and detailed planning and reviewing of special educational provision.

7. The protection of the special educational provision specified in a Statement requires:
   a. ensuring through inspection that LEAs fulfil their duties to review their arrangements for special educational provision, perhaps by OFSTED or some other agency like the Audit Commission;
   b. greater specification of duties on schools (see 10 below);
   c. the tightening of the appeals system to make tribunal judgements binding, subject to further appeal.

The duties under the Education Acts 1944 (section 8) and 1981 (section 2) provide the statutory starting points for protection and would need to be specified in more detail.

8. A dual system of assessment and decision making would give parents an option, either
   a. for quicker and more efficient decision making when there is agreement between the parties involved (*required assessment* and a simple *record* of special educational provision), or
   b. to use the existing decision making system when there are disagreements for adjudicating (*full statutory assessment* and maintaining *Statements*).

9. Regulations are needed to establish the shorter system of decision making and link it to the duty on LEAs to make the specific provision available.

10. Some of the duties now applying to LEAs in the 1981 Act should also apply to school governing bodies. For example, section 2(1) of the Act places a duty on LEAs to secure provision, whereas the duty on governors in 2(5)a is to use their 'best endeavour'. This requirement on governing bodies should be replaced by a straight duty as in section 2(1). This would mirror the extension of management and financial responsibilities and powers to school governing bodies, adding corresponding duties for special educational needs.

11. There is also a need for central guidance to clarify the conditions under which children with special educational needs will be educated in ordinary schools.

REFERENCES

Audit Commission/HMI (1992), *Getting in on the Act*. London: HMSO.

Cox, B., (1981), *The Law of Special Educational Needs: a guide to the Education Act 1981*. London: Croom Helm.

Department of Education and Science (DES) (1978), *Special Educational Needs* (Warnock Report). London: HMSO.

Department of Education and Science (DES) (1981), The Education Act 1981. *Circular 8/81*.

Department of Education and Science (DES), (1983) Assessments and statements of special educational needs. *Circular 1/83*.

Department of Education and Science (DES) (1989a), Assessments and statements of special educational needs. *Circular 22/89*.

Department of Education and Science (DES) (1989), *From Policy to Practice*.

Department of Education and Science (DES) (1991a), *The Parent's Charter. You and your children's education*.

Department of Education and Science (DES) (1991b), Local management of schools: further guidance. *Circular 7/91*.

Department for Education (DFE) (1992a), *Special Educational Needs: access to the system*. Consultation Paper.

Department for Education (DFE) (1992b), *Choice and Diversity: a new framework for schools*. Cm 2021. London: HMSO.

Dessent, T., (1987), *Making the Ordinary School Special*. London: Falmer Press.

Goacher, B., Evans. J., Welton, J. and Wedell, K., (1988), *Policy and Provision for Special Educational Needs*. London: Cassell.

National Curriculum Council (1989), *A Curriculum for All; special educational needs in the National Curriculum*. York: National Curriculum Council.

Norwich (1990), *Reappraising Special Needs Education*. London: Cassell.

O'Hear, P. and White, J. (1990), *A National Curriculum for All: laying the foundations for success*. Education and Training Paper No.6. London: Institute for Public Policy Research.

Pumfrey, P. and Mittler, P. (1989), Peeling off the label. *The Times Educational Supplement* 13 October.

Select Committee Report (1987) *Special Educational Needs: implementation of the Education Act 1981* (Education, Arts and Science Committee), London: HMSO

Warnock, M., (1991) House of Lords debate on special educational needs. Hansard, Vol DXXXII, October-November, p.971.

Wedell, K., (1983) Assessing special educational needs, *Secondary Educational Journal*, *13*, 14-16

Wedell, K., (1990), The 1988 Act and current principles of special educational needs, in Daniels, H. and Ware, J., *Special Educational Needs and the National Curriculum*. London: Kogan Page in association with the Institute of Education, University of London.

Wedell, K., (1991), A question of assessment, *British Journal of Special Education*, *18*, 1, 4-7